John Train

The
ORANGE
Golden Joy

PHOTOGRAPHY BY
Mark E. Smith

DISTRIBUTED BY
ANTIQUE COLLECTORS' CLUB

EASTHAMPTON, MA　　　　　　　　　　WOODBRIDGE, U.K.

Thanks are due to the staff of the Oscar Tintori
greenhouse for their generous advice, to Maria
Teresa Train for major research and to Katherine
Manisco for making her works available.

J.T.

Design by: Natasha Tibbott, Our Designs, Inc.

Prepress and Printing: ZoneS, Milano

ISBN 1 85149 525 8

Cover art by Rita Luskovic.

INTRODUCTION

By Francis H. Cabot

Founder, The Garden Conservancy

Robespierre, we are told, lost some of his revolutionary credentials, and was indeed denounced a "sybarite," because of his devotion to "pyramids" of oranges. Not to the point of having one's head chopped off, one can nevertheless sympathize. Is there anything quite so good as the taste of the juice of Valencia oranges squeezed just before breakfast on a spring morning, or as overpowering as the scent of citrus blossoms in a garden or an orangerie? And marmalade. What enchantment! I have heard that Seville oranges were floated from their transports into Scottish harbors, thus acquiring the special flavor of that product.

John Train and Mark Smith have given us an informative and well-illustrated treatise on the "golden fruit" that illuminates its origins and gradual spread throughout the world, its prevalence in mosque and palace gardens, its healthgiving attributes and its importance as a symbol in painting and sculpture. The book also tells how to plant and maintain a tree in one's home, as well as the complexities of bringing a commercial crop to market.

In addition, there are recipes for the use of citrus in food and drink, and a helpful compendium of the most important species and varieties.

Readers will find THE ORANGE informative, entertaining and useful: a delight.

View from Positano.

THE ORANGE: GOLDEN JOY

*Do you know the land
where the lemon trees bloom?*

"Kennst du das Land
wo die Zitronen blühn?"

Goethe

FOREWORD

From its first appearance in the western world, carried back from Asia by Alexander the Great, the orange and its cousins have brought delight. The orange started in ancient times as a much-loved decorative plant, and then, along with the lemon, became an element in eating and drinking. As lime, it was for centuries the cure for that bane of mariners, scurvy.

Only in recent times has it become a standard foodstuff, particularly its juice, which many of us enjoy every morning. I can't prove it, but I feel that the breakfast glass of orange juice is not only a most pleasant way to start the day but somehow highly beneficial. Of course, pleasure is itself already beneficial, but I think there's more to it than that.

Among the joys of living at this time in the history of the world are not having to clank around in armor or lug a heavy weapon, the ready availability of books, effective pharmaceuticals if we get sick, and good food to help us stay healthy in the first place. For me, the morning *fresh* orange juice is well up in the latter category.

Originally though, people treasured citrus for decoration. This book offers suggestions as to some varieties that have been found successful, including a few that flourish indoors. At home we have a splendid old lemon bush that lives indoors in winter, looks and smells delightful, and has blossomed and borne fruit for 50 years!

In this volume I often use the word orange to invoke citrus in general: both the bitter orange (now mostly decorative and for marmalade) and the delicious sweet orange, plus the mandarin, citron, lemon, lime, grapefruit, bergamot, tangerine, tangelo, and the rest. Also the innumerable excellent new varieties produced by natural or artificial cross-breeding. The back of the book describes a few of the main varieties, but there are many, many more, and new ones every day.

Print from Florilegium by Basilius Belser (1613). From left: Citron, Seville Orange, Orange.

ORIGINS

He hangs in shade the orange bright
Like golden lamps in a green light.

Marvell

History is embodied in names. As to the orange, both fruit and word probably originated many millennia ago in northern India, where it still grows wild. The word is an example of the migrating "N." Sanskrit naranga or narungo became Hindustani narungee, Italian arancia (Latinized as aurantium) and Spanish naranja. So it could have been a norange in English, instead of an orange, the way Shakespeare has a nuncle for our an uncle.

And why citrus? The yellow-green core of the cedar of Lebanon looks about like the citron, a cousin of the orange, which by mistake was thus called cedar: kedro in Greek or citreum in Latin, or citrus in English. In Italian the word cedro is still used for both cedar and citron. Incidentally, orchard comes from Latin hortus, garden, whence a hort-yard, later orchard.

Citrus made its way to the Arab and Roman worlds on the usual currents of trade and war. Like Napoleon in Egypt, Alexander the Great brought scientists along on his conquests, who noticed the citron, and brought it back to Asia Minor, whence it reached the Mediterranean countries. Then, the Arabs carried it west with their armies in the eighth and ninth centuries.

The Moorish conquest of Southern Spain brought with it the bitter orange, which still grows there, and is thus often known as the Seville orange. Its bitter rind, which is mixed with the pulp, makes for excellent marmalade. My own view is that the quantity of rind is central to good marmalade, which for reasons I do not fully grasp often comes from Scotland.

Theophrastus mentions citrus in 300 BC, as does Virgil, in the Georgics. The Hebrews involved it in rituals, and it is even found on their coinage and funerary monuments. They took the citron with them on their diaspora in the first century AD, and planted it where they went. A cookbook by Apicius in the first century AD mentions the *Citrus medica*. The first stop for citrus on the way from the middle east to central Italy was probably the south, Calabria, because of its geographical position and warm climate; then on up the peninsula. Lemons are shown in ancient Roman mosaics and frescos.

Orange tree in front of the Cathedral of Granada, Spain

Like so much else, the culture of the citrus died out in Europe in the dark ages, until reintroduced in the tenth century. The crusaders became familiar with it, as noted by Bishop Jacques de Vitry in his history. When the Arabs entered Sicily they brought the bitter orange, *Citrus aurantium*, which they disseminated commercially to southern Europe.

On two occasions oranges tempted foreign powers to invade Italy.

In the first, a Byzantine ruler recalled his governor of Rome, who, furious, sent an offering of Italian oranges to the king of the Lombards with an invitation to take over, which was accepted with alacrity. In the second, the Prince of Salerno, threatened by Arab attacks, sent a spectacular offering of oranges to the Duke of Normandy, urging him to occupy southern Italy. The Duke thought that was a fine idea, and snapped up Sicily into the bargain. The Norman-Arab culture that then arose became one of the wonders of Europe.

The Portuguese in China, who in addition to their religion, carried much of interest to the east, such as clocks, prisms, three-dimensional paintings and world globes, also brought home a vast assortment of plants, of which the Portuguese bitter orange was the most important. It went from there to the Middle East, whence its Arabic name, bortukan, i.e., "Portugal," Arabic being without a "p."

Later, the sweet orange, tastier than the Portuguese version, reached Europe from China, whence its present-day botanical name, *Citrus sinensis*.

Columbus introduced the bitter orange to our continent, and Pizarro to Peru. The orange seeds that Columbus planted in Hispaniola proliferated wonderfully throughout the Caribbean. Twenty years later Ponce de Leon carried the fruit to Florida, and followed up with more on his voyage of 1539. (It is said that seeking the Fountain of Youth, he instead brought it.) It so prospered that Spain obliged its ships headed for America to bring first seeds and then small trees to plant on each voyage, all for medical purposes. Today, Florida grows a quarter of the world's oranges, of many varieties, almost entirely for juice production. The Indian River fruit is considered the best of all.

Around 1769 the Franciscan fathers in San Diego introduced the sweet orange, *Citrus sinensis*, which they had brought with them when they came up from Mexico to found their California missions. Here again, the introduction was prodigiously successful: that state comes after Florida as America's largest citrus producer, followed by Arizona and Texas. The drier climate of California is more adapted to thick-skinned fruit that are better to eat, while Florida, with its sandy soil and hot damp climate, grows thin-skinned oranges prized for their juice.

The grapefruit was carried to the new world in 1806 by Count Odet Philippe, who planted a grove near Tampa in 1823. Florida remains the world's primary grapefruit producer.

Citrus grows in many places abroad, such as Spain, Sicily, Morocco, Tunisia, and Israel, but the lemon paradise is the Amalfi Coast and Sorrento, where Goethe wrote his famous poem of which a fragment serves as epigraph to this volume: Kennst du das Land.... When the lemon trees there are indeed in bloom (at the same time they are bearing fruit) their fragrance fills the countryside. The plantations sometimes follow the contour of the coast, which means that they slope steeply down to the sea, protected from the elements by wooden trellises overhead as protection in the event of high wind, snow or heat.

ABOVE: *First century fresco depicting birds in citrus tree from "La Casa del Frutteto," Pompeii.*

BELOW: *"Oranges in a Basket." oil painting by Gunvor Hellström.*

GARDEN OF THE HESPERIDES

To the strand the daughters of the sunset
The apple-tree, the singing and the gold.

Euripides, "Hippolitus"

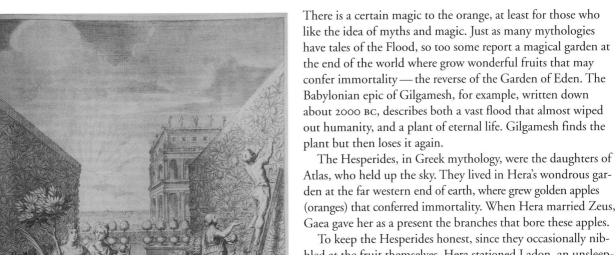

There is a certain magic to the orange, at least for those who like the idea of myths and magic. Just as many mythologies have tales of the Flood, so too some report a magical garden at the end of the world where grow wonderful fruits that may confer immortality — the reverse of the Garden of Eden. The Babylonian epic of Gilgamesh, for example, written down about 2000 BC, describes both a vast flood that almost wiped out humanity, and a plant of eternal life. Gilgamesh finds the plant but then loses it again.

The Hesperides, in Greek mythology, were the daughters of Atlas, who held up the sky. They lived in Hera's wondrous garden at the far western end of earth, where grew golden apples (oranges) that conferred immortality. When Hera married Zeus, Gaea gave her as a present the branches that bore these apples.

To keep the Hesperides honest, since they occasionally nibbled at the fruit themselves, Hera stationed Ladon, an unsleeping dragon with a hundred heads.

Hercules, as a penance for killing his family in a fit of madness, was assigned twelve labors, of which the last was to snatch the golden apples. This he did by persuading Prometheus (or the sea-god Nereus) to tell him where the garden was found. Hercules then induced Atlas, the father of the Hesperides, to collect some of the apples, offering to take his place holding up the sky while he did it. In some versions Hercules kills Ladon; in others he kills Antaeus, son of Gaea, by holding him away from his fortifying mother, the earth. In any event, he made off to Greece with some of the apples, but Athena eventually returned them to the garden… rather like the Gilgamesh story.

The Hesperides are usually given as three, Hesperia (representing night), Aegle ("Dazzling Light," associated with the citron),

"The Nymphs, Custodians of Citrus." Engraving from "Hesperides," by G. B. Ferrari, 1646. In this engraving citrus cultivation is personified in its mytical and devine origin. The three Hesperides nymphs are depicted as follows: Arethusa offers an orange, Dedalus is grafting a lemon tree, while Hesperia is supervising. Cosmo prunes a citrus plant admired by Aegle, while Alcimo is planting an orange tree.

FOLOWING PAGE: *View of terraced grove, Amalfi Coast.*

and Arethusa (with the lemon). They are sometimes also called the Daughters of the Evening, the Daughters of the Sunset or the Western Maidens. They loved to sing. Hesperus, their grandfather, personifies evening and is the name of the evening star.

But where was the famous Garden? It's no easy matter to locate a mythical place, such as the garden of Eden or the entrance to Hades. Many authorities placed it among the warm islands of the eastern Atlantic, or on the West African coast — whether Mauritania (as maintained by the great naturalist Pliny) — Senegal (urged da Mosto, who claimed to have seen it) or Egypt or elsewhere. In any event, in a mild climate, suitable for citrus.

Renaissance mapmakers moved the garden to all sorts of locations. Over time it became more than just an orchard, and assumed spiritual qualities. As a result the idea of the orangery became favored by the Church, which already liked the spiritual symbolism of the garden.

THE HOUSE OF ORANGE

What about the royal House of Orange and the Irish Orangemen? The name of Arausia, a Roman town on the Rhone in the Vaucluse area of southern France, slowly evolved into Aurengia, then Orenge and finally Orange. In the twelfth century it became the capital of a principality. A Prince of Orange received for his services a substantial bit of the low countries from Charles V, the Holy Roman Emperor. An heir of the last prince, Philibert, was William the Silent of Nassau, Prince of Orange and head of the ruling family of the Netherlands, in whose honor Dutch explorers named South Africa's Orange River. His grandson, William II, married Mary, daughter of Charles I of England, producing King William III of England. The Orange Lodge of Freemansons was named for William III, who ousted his father-in-law, James II, in the "Glorious Revolution" of 1688. The resemblance of the name of the house to the color of the fruit led the supporters of William III to display orange scarves and ribbons to show their support for Protestantism in Ireland. The Orangemen, as they were called, were ultra-Protestants of Ulster.

Decorated sideboard in dining room, Vaux-le-Vicomte, France.

GARDENS AND ORANGERIES

Engravings from "Hesperides" by G. B. Ferrari (1646), depicting two Orangeries.

GARDEN OF THE NUNS

I stole this orange from the garden of the nuns
to bring to you Juanita.
It dropped between the shining leaves,
and I reached down to pick it up
as the sisters meditated, behind draperies
and cool windowpanes, on the Acts of the Apostles.
And yes Juanita, there are more oranges for you
from the garden of the nuns. This
orange I bring to you
to release you from your own meditations,
the ones that haunt you.
Take this orange, Juanita. It holds the sun.

George Wallace

Lemons… glossy-leafed and fragrant… in huge seventeenth-century jars of dusty terra cotta of which such care was taken that they were carried out from the vast old lemon-house in the spring, and back there in the late autumn, when they were further protected by scaffolds hung with screens of straw… spangled with ivory-white buds and rosettes of gold-flecked, perfumed blossom, as well as bearing fruit at every stage, from small, dark shapes, no bigger than a hazel-nut, to fruit of green bronze, and then gradually coloured and shaped by the sun, to the finely-drawn elliptical ripe lemon, painted with so gay a brush…

From "Great Morning" by Osbert Sitwell

For more than a thousand years after it reached Europe, the orange was chiefly enjoyed as decoration.

Boccaccio, in the Decameron, which appeared in 1350, offers the first descriptions of orangeries in Tuscany. Francesco Colonna speaks of orange, lemon and citron trees in his 1464 description of gardens in Lombardy and the Veneto.

The prodigious mosque of Cordoba, erected in the ninth and tenth centuries by Abd Al-Rahman I and II, follows a remarkable plan: the "Patio de los Naranjos," or outside orangery, repeats the pattern of the columns that support it inside. It is one of the great sights of Europe. The Mosque of Seville, founded by Calib Abn Ya'eub Yusuf, followed the same layout. Seville's streets are lined with wonderful orange trees, the way other cities have plane trees or chestnuts.

The Almohad empire loved huge irrigated gardens, as found in Marrakech, Rabat and Gibraltar.

Boccaccio describes an "amazingly beautiful" suburban garden whose center is surrounded by a line of green orange and lemon trees which offer shade and a delightful aroma.

The Citrus Cloister, Church of Badia, Florence. (Photo Fratelli Alinari)

Lorenzo Valla praises the sublime Moorish gardens of Valencia, where flourished many varieties of citrus. This depiction helped inspire Cosimo the Elder to create a garden at his villa at Fiesole. The fifteenth century Medici took up citrus cultivation in a very big way indeed, including Lorenzo il Magnifico's Agnano gardens in Pisa, and, in the early 16 century, Archduke Cosimo's garden of the Villa di Castello.

Niccoló Pericoli, "Il Tribolo," who designed this garden, also designed the prodigious Medici gardens at the Palazzo Pitti in Florence (acquired in 1549 from the Pitti family), later carried forward under the guidance of Fontini, Vasari, Ammannati and Buontalenti. After the cadet line of the Medici family died out, the Habsburg dynasty succeeded them as Archdukes and restored and expanded the gardens, including the Limonaia (1777–1778) by del Lorena. In 2004, thanks to the support of the Italian Government and the World Monuments Fund of New York (of which the author had been a director), the refurbished Limonaia opened again after two years of reconstruction. The local newpapers gushed — rightly — over the "sublime harmony" of the installation.

Perhaps the greatest of all orange gardens was at Villa di Castello, between Florence and Sesto Fiorentino. When the senior branch of the Medici dried out, the cadet branch, starting with Giovanni dalle Bande Nere, assumed the primacy of Florence. Giovanni, the finest soldier of sixteenth century Italy, called "of the Black Bands" for the color of his troops' uniforms, grew up in Castello. He was a robust, lovable man, who sought to toughen his infant son Cosimo by tossing him from a battlement into waiting arms (observed, with horror, we may assume, by the child's mother, Maria Salviati). After Giovanni died at the battle of Pavia, Cosimo, later the first Grand Duke of Tuscany, became head of the family, ruling from an early age with a cruel severity unknown to his predecessors.

To show his ability to create order and beauty, in a garden as in a domain, Cosimo had irrigation water carried down through canals into fountains that represented the Tuscan landscape until they reached the two main fountains of the Giardino Grande. One of these was adorned with a bronze group of Hercules and Antaeus. (See the section on the Garden of the Hesperides.)

Succeeding Medici generations improved this famous garden, which exhibited hundreds of potted citrus specimens, some developed by the family itself.

When Charles VIII of France marched into Italy bent on conquest he was, like so many, overwhelmed instead by Italian culture, its art, its beautiful buildings and their magnificent interiors, and the cultivated oranges that embellished their grounds. At his chateau at Amboise, which under his successor Francis I housed Leonardo da Vinci, Charles erected the first large greenhouse intended specifically for oranges, an orangerie. (The very earliest, smaller, seems to date from 1336.)

His queen followed suit at her own chateau at Blois, and thereafter few royal and noble palaces were complete without their own increasingly splendid orangeries, culminating in the magnificent one designed by Mansart for Louis XIV at Versailles in 1764. It was in the shape of a square with one side missing, over a thousand feet around. He used it as an indoor pleasure-garden, the site of receptions and balls. Louis XIV favored as an aphrodisiac a concoction of orange, spirits and sugar."*

Two queens of France, Catherine and then Marie de Medici, were Italian, and brought with them the fondness for oranges, orangeries and orange decoration of their native land. About 1820 the French custom of providing orange blossoms for a bride passed to England. Few trees are more prolific than the orange, so its flower symbolized fertility, while its white blossoms represented innocence (as in Japan, incidentally). Thus, in England, "gathering orange blossoms" meant seeking a bride.

* His physician once noticed that the King seemed debilitated and told him to avoid aphrodisiacs until further notice. Some time later, finding him still debilitated, the medico asked if he had indeed avoided aphrodisiacs. "Yes," replied the monarch: "although just for variety, a few visits to the Parc aux Cerfs" (his private brothel). "Ahah," replied the physician, "but variety is the *greatest* aphrodisiac." When Louis was 70, his wife, some years older, wrote the Bishop of Chartres to ask if she had to submit to his desires twice a day. Yes, the word came back, as a good wife, and to help him avoid sin, she must submit.

Ornamental orange trees bordering Plaza del Triunfo, Seville.

ABOVE: *Shönbrunn, the Orangerie. Vienna, in winter.*
(Photo by Lisa Train)

OPPOSITE PAGE: *Versailles, the Orangerie. The*
square wooden pots with one hinged side to
facilitate changing the soil and trimming the
roots, are a French invention, first seen here.

Kumquat tree in the Alcazar Gardens, Seville.

A view of the reflecting pools surrounded by ornamental orange and lemon trees. Alcazar Gardens, Seville.

OPPOSITE PAGE: *Patio entrance to the garden of the palace of the Duke of Alba, Seville.* ABOVE: *The same garden, famous for its varieties of citrus.*

BELOW: *Orange trees in the vaulted terrace of Casa de Pilatos. Seville.*

21

*"Patio de los Naranjas," Cordoba Cathedral.
The orange trees are planted to repeat the
pattern of the columns inside the cathedral.*

VILLA MEDICI DI CASTELLO

This garden was designed in the early sixteenth century to favor the cultivation of citrus fruits, whether in a pot or espaliered. One of the most important collections of potted fruit trees in the world, it boasts five hundred specimens, some of which are rare examples descending from varieties cultivated by the Medici.

ABOVE: *One of the four paintings depicting citrus fruits by Bartolomeo Bimbi. These were commissioned by the Medici family, between 1696–1699. All 116 citrus fruits known at the time are depicted in this series.*

OPPOSITE PAGE: *A view of the citrus garden with statuary.*

FOLLOWING PAGE: *View of the same citrus garden with the greenhouse in the background.*

Citron Cedrat or Rough Lemon, watercolor by Katherine Manisco, a Fellow of the Linnean Society of London and a Member of the Prince of Wale's Highgrove Florilegium. An exhibition of her watercolors was part of the 2004 Limonaia at Boboli Gardens reopening celebration.

Boboli Gardens at Palazzo Pitti

The "Giardino di Boboli" is one of the most famous museum gardens in the world and in Renaissance history. These gardens were designed by the architect Niccoló Pericoli, known as "Il Tribolo," under the auspices of Eleonora di Toledo, wife of Cosimo de Medici, in 1549. These formal gardens have continued to be expanded and become home to a vast collection of exotic plants. In 1777 Grand Duke Peter Leopold de Lorraine organized the restoration of the gardens and added the citrus greenhouse or Limonaia, designed by Zanobi del Rosso.

This structure was restored in 2004 and today houses many of the original varieties.

Entrance to the Limonaia.
BELOW: *View of the lake with traditional terracotta pots containing lemon trees.*

ABOVE: *"Vasca dell'Isola," by Giambologna (1576).*

OPPOSITE PAGE: *"Fontana dell'Oceano." Both
fountains are surrounded by potted lemon trees.*

VILLA REALE DI MARLIA

Villa Reale di Marlia, near Lucca, was first built in the fifteenth century by the Buonvisi family. Napoleon's sister, Elisa Baciocchi, made Villa Reale her home in 1805. The "Giardino dei Limoni" is beautifully arranged in four rectangles, each one having a central magnolia surrounded by lemon trees. At one end is "La Peschiera," with its allegorical statues of the rivers Arno and Serchio.

ABOVE: *"La Peschiera," with the statues of the rivers Arno and Serchio by the grotto.*

OPPOSITE PAGE: *"La Peschiera" by the lemon garden. Watercolors by John Sargent.*

33

LE SIRENUSE HOTEL, POSITANO

The old palazzo of the Marchese Sersale was converted into the Sirenuse Hotel in 1951. This beautiful hotel, owned and managed by the Sersale family, overlooks the Island of the Sirens, and to this day is one of the most elegant in Southern Italy.

ABOVE: *Dining room decorated with citrus trees.*

BELOW: *Corner of the garden.*

OPPOSITE PAGE: *View of the swimming pool with mosaic grotto.*

THE ORANGE IN ART

When Constantinople fell to the Turks in 1453, there was a general flight to the West. Many of the eminent migrated to Florence, and to Lorenzo de Medici's Academy. Like numerous other rulers, Il Magnifico took pride in his assemblage of the learned, notably the humanists (classical scholars), such as Pico della Mirandola. They were paid extremely generously, like today's media stars, and were indeed a lasting adornment to their city and their patron.

Thus, when Benozzo Gozzoli wanted to celebrate the family in the marvelous Medici Chapel, he employed a triple metaphor: the Journey of the Magi, with Gaspar, Balthasar, and Melchior (representing the fugitives from Constantinople) riding through the Tuscan countryside. They, in turn, symbolized Lorenzo (with a young and handsome countenance substituted for his actual somber visage), Emperor of the East John Paleologus and Patriarch Joseph. In addition are depicted other members of the family, Benozzo himself, and, transformed into a frivolous youth, the fearsome Castruccio Castracani, war leader of Lucca, Florence's perennial foe. Surrounding the scene are extensive orange groves, although at the time of Jesus' birth, the occasion of the Biblical Journey of the Magi, oranges were not found in the Holy Land.

The same fallacy pervaded Italian Renaissance art. Many flights into Egypt are through orange groves. Fra Angelico, Duccio and Ghirlandaio all show oranges in the Holy Land, where none actually grew.

Similarly, many pictures of Mary were embellished with oranges, since the fruit had to some extent become her personal symbol.

The Medici patronized Botticelli, whose "Primavera" depicts a beautified Giuliano dei Medici transformed into Mercury, somewhat improbably harvesting oranges. Botticelli's "Birth of Venus" depicts the goddess genteelly wafted ashore aboard a scallop shell to a strand bedecked with orange trees.

Not surprisingly, the ceilings of the Palazzo Pitti, where dwelt Cosimo the first Grand Duke, were embellished with oranges.

It has been argued that the famous five — later, six — palle or balls of the Medici crest were originally oranges. It may also be that they acquired this motif from the Lombards, a Frankish tribe (called Langobardi — long-haired — by the Romans) who moved from Germany to the Po in northern Italy — the Lombard Empire. The Lombards were overthrown by Charlemagne and scattered around Europe. They settled in London as moneylenders, with the pawnbroker's three balls as their symbol.

First century fresco depicting a citrus tree. Pompeii.

Detail of "The Last Judgment," by Fra Angelico (circa 1431), Museo di San Marco, Florence. (Photo Fratelli Alinari)

Detail of "The Procession of the Magi," by
Benozzo Gozzoli (1459), Palazzo Medici-Riccardi,
Florence.
(Photo Fratelli Alinari)

"Adoration of the Child with St. John," glazed terracotta by Giovanni della Robbia (1490–1530) Museo del Bargello, Florence. (Photo Fratelli Alinari)

"Last Supper," by Ghirlandaio (1480), Museo di San Marco, Florence. (Photo Fratelli Alinari)

Detail of "Primavera," by Sandro Botticelli (1417).
Uffizi Gallery, Florence.
(Photo Fratelli Alinari)

Detail of "Madonna with Child," by Andrea Mantegna
(1457–1459). Church of San Zeno Maggiore, Verona.
(Photo Fratelli Alinari)

Detail of fresco in The Bridal Chamber, Palazzo Ducale, Mantua,
by Andrea Mantegna (1465–1474).
(Photo Fratelli Alinari)

"Madonna del Limone" by Paolo Cavazzolo, also called Il Morando (1486–1522).

"Children Picking Fruit" by Francisco Goya (1746–1828) Prado Museum, Madrid.

BELOW: *"La Merienda" by Francisco Goya (1746–1828) Prado Museum, Madrid.*

"Orange Fruit" by Luis E. Melendez (1716–1780), Prado Museum, Madrid.

Detail of "Still Life with Drapery" by Paul Cezanne, (1899), The Hermitage, St. Petersburg.

A citrus grove protected by a wooden trellis, typically used along the Amalfi Coast. Oil painting by Cristina Cini.

CITRUS ON SHIPBOARD

Perhaps the most precious single value of the orange — including its cousins — has been for the mariner, as a cure for scurvy: in technical language, as an anti-scorbutic.

Scurvy always used to beset sailors on voyages that were too long for perishable foods, notably greens, to survive. It arises from a lack of Vitamin C, found in citrus and certain vegetables, and produces horrible symptoms: the gums bleed, the teeth and hair fall out, bones break, capillaries hemorrhage into the tissues and the sufferer grows weaker and weaker. On Vasco da Gama's first cruise around the Cape of Good Hope just at the end of the fifteenth century, half his crew died miserably of scurvy.

Once a year a huge Spanish ship, the "Manila Galleon," sailed between the Philippines and Lima, Peru. By the end of the voyage the crew were sometimes so debilitated by scurvy that they could no longer work the ship, which, its sails set for its course, thus plowed right on past its destination, unable to make the turn into port, and vanished. Only in the eighteenth century was it widely understood that citrus, rich in Vitamin C, was an efficient cure. Late in the century the British started distributing regular rations of lime juice to their sailors (whence "Limeys"), solving the problem.

When the antiscorbutic merits of citrus became established, its spread accelerated. Portuguese mariners planted trees along their new trade routes to the orient: on Madeira, the Azores, West Africa and St. Helena. The Spanish followed suit, as did the Dutch in South Africa.

Since the benefits of citrus in combating scurvy were so spectacular, physicians reasoned that it must possess general therapeutic value, and so prescribed it for a wide variety of complaints, such as stomach trouble, worms, impotence and even poisoning. (Note the many "medica" variations, in the final section.) Some desperate enthusiasts prescribed it for that terrifying menace, the black death…unsuccessfully, alas.

Open market display of lemons and cherry tomatoes.

Orange and lemon sellers in the harbor of Mils, Sardinia. 18th century print. (Photo Fratelli Alinari)

Citrus perfumes, soaps, cosmetics and liquors have been produced for centuries by the "Officina Profumo – Farmaceutica di Santa Maria Novella," Florence.

THE MANY USES OF CITRUS

We tend to overlook the many everyday uses of citrus. For instance, cleaning products are laced with lemon to make things smell fresh.

Leftover rinds, pulp and seeds can be turned into molasses and added to cattle feed. The skins can be used by farmers as a soil conditioner.

More important, though, are the uses of citrus in shampoo, skin cream, toothpaste, and of course perfumes, notably eau de cologne.

The original formulation of eau de cologne was twelve drops each of the essential oils of oranges, bergamot, citron neroli and rosemary, with a dram of Malabar cardamoms and a gallon of rectified spirits, all distilled together.

FLEUR D'ORANGER

LEFT: *Bride with orange blossoms. 18th century print.*

BELOW: *Citrus perfume and cosmetic laboratory in the Sorrento Profumi shop, Sorrento.*

Preparation of almonds for citrus candies. Lemon and orange candies.
BELOW: *Citrus products in the Confetti & Agrumetti shop, Sorrento.*

Lemon and orange candles, Sorrento.

BELOW: *Citrus candy. (Photo by Camilla McGrath)*

Packaged bottle of limoncello by Villa Massa, Sorrento.

"Limonoro" production and shop, Sorrento. Limonoro's limoncello is made from an ancient recipe and uses lemons freshly picked each morning. Limonoro also produces lemon cream and babamignon made from lemon cream and rum.

This charming 19th century wood statuette of a lemon vendor is displayed at Villa Massa's offices next to a modern factory where limoncello is produced and shipped all over the world.

A ceramic jar from the Amalfi region.

Spanish ceramic tile.

Ceramic tile depicting Positano.

Tapestry showing vase of oranges. Alcazar, the Mudejar Palace of the Spanish Kings, Seville.

Detail of pietra dura table top.

MARMALADE PRODUCTION
Marchesi di San Giuliano, Villasmundo, Sicily.

Slicing the fruits.

Starting production process.

The finished product.

Manuscript pages depicting a lemon and bitter orange harvest, from Codex Vindobonensis, fourteenth century. (Photo Fratelli Alinari)

CULTIVATING THE ORANGE

This is a most ancient subject. In 1179 the Chinese Han Yen Che wrote a "Treatise on Oranges" that sets forth appropriate varieties and techniques of breeding and cultivation and their medical use. Spanish Arabs, notably Ibn El Beithar of Malaga (1197–1248), Ibn Gurbair of Valencia (1183–1217) and Abu Zacaria of Seville (twelfth century) produced texts on the cultivation and use of citrus.

A prolific orange tree will produce many hundreds of fruits, or even a thousand, if the weather has been benign, and sometimes much more from a large tree. With luck, a tree can bear copiously for well over half a century.

The orange is often cultivated for its beauty and fragrance rather than to supply fruit for the table. For that in cool places you need a glassed-in conservatory or hothouse. A good small layout would have a central path and rows of pots along each side, set at ten

Sicilian orange grove.

Orange harvest in Sicily.

or twelve foot intervals. You may want hot water pipes near the surface for bottom heat, as it is called, although this is not necessary for growing flowers outdoors. Alternatively, you can grow the plant against a wall, covering it with mats in winter.

We can assume that you are buying a potted plant from a nursery. You might want to check the variety with the descriptions at the end of this volume to make sure that it's one of those that are happy in the conditions contemplated. Obviously, though, the nurseryman's opinions will be your primary guide.

He will doubtless suggest a program for watering and fertilizing, but here are some further comments.

Fertilizing

To begin with, you should spread a layer of organic fertilizer on top of the soil in the pot late during the winter, and from time to time add mineral fertilizer.

Some typical organic fertilizers are the following:

Manure. Dried horse manure is preferred. To discourage the transmission of fungi, it should not be placed too close to the trunk of the plant.

Another preferred fertilizer is whole or powdered lupin seeds, which contain nitrogen, the most important element in citrus nutrition. You can tell when nitrogen is lacking by the loss of vivid green in the plant's leaves. One needs enough nitrogen, which stimulates fruit production, but not too much, which creates excessive leaf growth at the expense of the fruit. If you buy the seeds whole, boil them before use, so that they won't germinate. You place the lupin seeds at the edge of the pot until they decompose. Then you push them a little way under the earth, but not in direct contact with the roots.

Ox blood, a rich source of nitrogen, is sold in packs that tell you how much should be applied. A little goes a long way.

Mineral fertilizers provide phosphorus, needed in spring and summer, potassium, which encourages the flavor and aroma of the fruit, iron, which fortifies the plant against fungi, magnesium, which stimulates chlorophyll production, and other trace elements. Complex fertilizers are available that provide most of what the plant needs.

Watering

You should feel the subsurface soil to see if it is dry or moist, and apply water accordingly. This ranges from every other day in summer, particularly if the plant moves outdoors, down to once a week or less in winter. If the leaves start to look sick, and particularly if they start to drop off, more water is needed. But avoid too much water in the plant's resting season.

A drip irrigation system is another good solution. Either way, you need to put stony fragments in the bottom of the pot to keep the bottom hole open. Standing water is disastrous for citrus.

The calamondrin seems to accept the dryness of an apartment about the best of any variety.

Repotting

This needs to be done for a young plant every two or three years, and for an older one every four to five years, to refresh the soil and let the roots grow out.

At the moment of repotting, the soil should be quite dry, so that lifting the plant out won't be too heavy a weight, and so that it will be easier to knock or scrape the old soil off the roots. Remember to put back shards around the drainage hole.

Incidentally, for myself, I greatly prefer terracotta pots to any other style, both as to looks, utility and tradition. Plastic is particularly unsatisfactory in that it does not breathe.

Pruning

Somewhat counterintuitively, the best shape for an orange tree growing outdoors is not neatly spherical, like a lightbulb, but with a thin spot on top to admit sunlight into the center of the plant, which otherwise will tend to dry up. This strengthens the plant and makes it more resistant to pests.

An ancient, tired but healthy tree is sometimes "skeletonized," meaning pruning all limbs thicker than one or two inches. The operation is performed early in spring, and results in no fruits for two years, followed by growth of exceptionally large ones.

After heavy pruning a citrus tree's bark is likely to suffer from sunburn, believe it or not, so one paints exposed areas with whitewash or thinned down water-based white paint.

Grafting

Many fruit trees should be developed by grafting; that is, you graft the variety you want to grow on to the rootstock best adapted to the place, and plant it as a seedling. Otherwise the tree will be spiny and irregular. So orange budwood may very well be grown on lemon rootstock. The bitter orange, brought by explorers and privateers, flourished marvelously in Florida and elsewhere, but is mainly used today as rootstock for the sweet orange. The rough lemon is currently the preferred rootstock, being somewhat less tasty but hardier and more resistant to pests.

Grove, with trellis and suspended storage hutch for protective coverings. From Il Pizzo lemon grove, Piana di Sorrento.

COMMERCIAL GROWING IN AMERICA

The orange you buy as fruit or juice will have been grown in a commercial grove. These run to considerable size. The one I had a connection with was about 5,000 acres: six times the size of Central Park in New York. That is a large affair, probably as big as a single manager should try to handle, assisted by a family member or two plus the regular employees and seasonal workers for the hard work of picking.

Let me say a word about agriculture in general. In the first place, what you grow is a commodity, not something you can get a patent on. You are thus competing with your neighbor and his hundreds or thousands of acres, and other farmers you may never see, from elsewhere in the country or abroad. Everybody is trying to produce the best quality at the lowest price. One would think that huge corporate farms would have an advantage, but in fact, they are weighed down by those layers of corporate overhead. Family farms are much more efficient; the boss can make better decisions on the spot; the employee/owners will make the necessary day and night continuous effort; and the younger generation will sacrifice current benefit for the long-term buildup of the assets.

You can become a high-tech specialist in the time it takes to get through MIT and put in a few years in a company lab, but there is essentially no such thing as a good first-generation farmer. You have to learn farming at your father's knee, since so much of the job is based on immemorially old techniques.

One unexpected feature of the agricultural game overall (not citrus) is its resemblance to a D-day landing. As with much of life, including babies, the creature waiting to be born increases enormously toward the end of the growing season: a potato doubles in size in the last few weeks, for instance. The growing season is defined as the time between the earliest moment when the earth is suitable for planting, and the last period before a killing frost is likely. So all the planting equipment has to be working perfectly at the beginning and all the harvesting machinery at the end. You want at least a 95% operability ratio, so that everything can happen in a rush, like getting a powerful force ashore on D-day. That means that all winter your maintenance shop is repairing and improving the equipment on a rigid schedule. During the harvest, when a combine, say, breaks down in the field at night, if your own crew has trouble fixing it, I've seen the manufacturer's maintenance team fly in from the next state in a light plane, land right there in the field, and work on the problem under arc lights until it was fixed. Try and get that service in a socialist system! (Soviet agriculture, I understand, was content with a 50% operability ratio. The incentives were wrong, political reliability came above management skill, and nothing worked.)

The farm ("ranch") in question was in Arizona, an environment unfriendly to pests, since it gets very hot and very cold, and is almost perfectly dry. The irrigation water came from the Colorado River. The trees consumed about six vertical feet of water a year.

Among the problems that a manager must be on top of day and night are keeping the people working fiendishly hard in the right slots, coping with plant diseases, juggling finances, monitoring the preventive maintenance schedule, replacing worn-out equipment, coping with government demands, shifting his sales strategy to cope with a changing market, and dealing with catastrophes of every description, including freezes.

To get a good price you have to position your output correctly. That starts with creating a brand, or usually several brands. A crate of citrus has a big label, just like a

bottle of wine, and the grower has to create an identity and then build loyalty to it.

On a big fresh fruit farm you have a packing house: essentially just a normal production line. The torrent of fruit comes in one door and is washed and sorted. The rejected culls are sent out to a juice plant. The good fruit then goes on to be treated, waxed, labeled and perhaps wrapped. Fruit with a label, such as "Sunkist," sells for a premium. Ripe oranges are often green in color when picked. If so, they are "sweated" to give them the proper color.

For a juice operation the fruit goes to a processing plant: washing, grading, and extracting the juice, which is then either pasteurized (for Not From Concentrate) or sent to the evaporator and freezer, for concentrate.

Speaking of juice, one of the peculiarities of the citrus world is that you can't get fresh juice in orange country. It's much more efficient to process the fruit as packaged juice or concentrate that an eatery can serve without further preparation, as against shipping the fruit to be cut and squeezed before being served. So you can ask high and low without success for fresh juice in orange country coffee shops or lunch counters. On the subject of nutrition, I should mention the Arizona orange country dinner. It seemed to consist of several glasses of whiskey, then a rubbery shrimp cocktail, then steak, then vanilla ice cream with chocolate sauce, and as a climax, a glass of red wine.

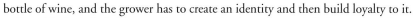

Anyway, the U.S. grows about 25 billion oranges a year, mostly in Florida and California. Florida oranges are juicier and sweeter, and about 80% used for juice, while California oranges have thicker skins but are less juicy. About 80% are destined for the table. Brazil grows about twice the quantity of Florida, in similar varieties and quality, but being in the southern hemisphere, in a complementary season: from July through January, while Florida produces from November through June.

Oranges are picked by hand, a hot, uncomfortable job. (Mechanical harvesters exist, which work by shaking the whole tree like a terrier shaking a rat, but they aren't popular.) The picked oranges are dropped into tubs holding about 900 pounds of fruit. A truck known as a "goat" comes along, picks up the tub with a hydraulic lift, and empties it into its cargo space. The goat then carries the fruit to an open tractor-trailer holding about 22 tons of fruit, which then goes to the processing plant. There, the fruit waits in gigantic bins, holding millions of oranges, to be processed into juice.

The rule right across agriculture seems to be that the warmer the climate the faster the growth, but the more profuse the pests. The tropical fruit fly, for instance, is a frightful hazard in Florida and points south. Others are root-rot (mal di gomma in Italy), cladosporium, which generates warty growths, and purple scale. Appropriate spraying or syringing helps keep the pests under control. Another interesting way of coping with this problem is to grow the fruit where pests are unhappy, such as in the Arizona desert, where the winters get so cold that the pests have a hard time… as, sometimes, do the trees themselves. Cold damage depends in part on the length of the exposure: A short dose will kill fruit; more, the branches; and a great deal, the whole tree. When orange growers learn of an approaching freeze they prepare counter-measures: smudge-pots, burning old tires, and even chartering a helicopter to blow the warmer air from above (the "temperature inversion" phenomenon) down to break up the freezing air at tree level.

COOKING WITH CITRUS

SUNDAY MORNING

Complacencies of the peignoir, and late

Coffee and oranges in a sunny chair,

And the green freedom of a cockatoo

Upon a rug mingle to dissipate

The holy hush of ancient sacrifice.

Wallace Stevens

Citrus was used in antiquity for cooking, although not for desserts. Its earliest popularity in Europe was based on its ornamental quality, and at table as a seasoning for meat and fish.

Renaissance Italy used citrus fruit in cooking, but only in a noble or royal court. Catherine de Medici brought it to France for use in the kitchen. She also brought with her a Sicilian ice-cream maker.

Dinner guests could measure their importance in the regard of their hosts by the number of oranges that came to the table. A famous menu: In 1529, the Archbishop of Milan gave a sixteen-course dinner that included caviar and oranges fried with sugar and cinnamon, brill and sardines with slices of orange and lemon, a thousand oysters with pepper and oranges, lobster salad with citrons, sturgeon in aspic covered with orange juice, fried sparrows with oranges, individual salads containing citrons, orange fritters, a soufflé with raisins and pine nuts covered with sugar and orange juice, five hundred fried oysters with lemon slices, and candied peels of citrons and oranges.

Ceramic table designed by Carole Biagiotti for the Giotti Store, Florence.

FISH

No fish dish is complete without lemon juice or lemon wedges. Poached fish will taste better if one adds a lemon cut in half, a celery stick and a carrot to the cold salted water in which it is being poached. One can also add parsley or dill to the water, depending on the fish. Poached fish is best served with home-made mayonnaise whipped with abundant lemon juice.

To make mayonnaise you need to beat two egg yolks adding ½ a teaspoon of salt and a little white pepper. This can be done with an electric beater at medium speed. Then drop by drop, add ½ cup of olive oil. Now add juice of ½ lemon, still beating constantly, followed by another ½ cup of olive oil and the other ½ of lemon juice. If the mayonnaise curdles, beat one more egg yolk in another bowl and slowly add the curdled mayonnaise to the beaten yolk to form a new emulsion.

YING'S FAMOUS LOBSTER

My Chinese cook, Ying, makes a lobster that delights the Downeasters. The big difference is that she adds an orange quarter, lemon juice, a piece of ginger and a scallion to a tomato-based sauce with a touch of ketchup and teaspoon of sugar.

Incidentally, the Chinese, who know a lot, serve weak tea — one tea bag for three people — in fingerbowls after having lobster, which cuts the fishy grease much better than our usual water with mint or lemon.

MEAT

When serving stew or braised meat have a small dish of grenolata on the table to sprinkle on the meat. Grenolata is prepared with 1 part grated lemon zest, 1 part chopped garlic clove, and chopped parsley.

CHICKEN WITH LEMON

One young roasting chicken
One lemon
Olive oil, salt and pepper
Rosemary

Rub chicken inside and outside with a mixture of salt, pepper, olive oil and rosemary. Place a whole lemon, pierced with a fork, inside the chicken. Roast the chicken for approximately 30-40 minutes in a 350 degree preheated oven.

CHICKEN WITH ORANGE

Prepare as for chicken with lemon. Substitute one peeled orange divided in quarters for the lemon.

ORANGE DUCK

One medium-sized duck
Five oranges
Two spoonfuls of sugar
One small onion
One medium carrot
One celery stick
Olive oil, salt, pepper and sage
Half a glass of brandy
Half a glass of white wine
Olive oil, salt and pepper

There are many ways of preparing this dish. One is to fill the duck with half an orange cut in small pieces, plus a few sage leaves, salt and pepper. Bind the bird with string to attach the wings and legs to the body. Mix salt, pepper and oil and rub on the outside of the duck. Put it in a roasting pan in a medium warm oven for one and a half hours, turning the duck over. Add the brandy a few minutes before taking the duck out of the oven. Remove the duck.

Add to the sauce left in the pan all of the chopped vegetables. Put it on the stove, when the onions soften add the sugar and the peeled and sliced oranges; let it cook a few minutes and add the white wine. Pass this sauce through a sieve and return to the pan to cook for five minutes. Add the duck cut in four pieces to the pan, heat and serve with the sauce and decorate with orange slices.

HINTS

1. A bit of orange juice enhances avocado.

2. Orange with chocolate is irresistible.

3. Before squeezing a lemon, roll it, applying gentle pressure, on the kitchen table. That gives you more juice when you cut and squeeze it.

4. To keep orange juice fresh overnight, so it won't lose its flavor or degrade its vitamin C content, store the juice (not the fruit itself) in the refrigerator, in a sealed container.

5. The heaviest fruits contain the most juice.

6. If it doesn't look healthy, it may not be fresh.

Cutlets
Bread crumbs
Eggs
Butter
Olive oil, salt and pepper
Lemons

Pound the cutlets to flatten. Add lemon juice, salt and pepper to the lightly beaten eggs and put in a flat dish, in which you will dip the cutlets. Then sprinkle them on both sides with abundant grated bread. Melt the butter and oil in a skillet. When hot, add the seasoned cutlets to fry. Turn them over once and when ready place them on paper to absorb the extra fat. Serve with lemon wedges to be squeezed on the cutlets at the table.

SALADS

Many salads are enhanced by adding slices or dices of citrus fruit.

FENNEL AND ORANGE SALAD

One medium fennel
Two oranges
Black olives
Half small red onion
Watercress or similar green salad
Olive oil, salt and pepper
Half spoon of lemon juice

Slice the fennel and the onion in thin circles, add the black olives and watercress. Peel and cut oranges in sections, removing the pith. Mix all in a salad bowl and make a dressing with the remaining ingredients.

AVOCADO AND GRAPEFRUIT SALAD

One avocado
One celery stick
Half sweet onion
One grapefruit
Olive oil, salt and pepper
Balsamic vinegar

Slice the avocado, cut the onion in thin circles, dice the celery. Peel the grapefruit, cut it in sections and remove the pith. Mix all in a salad bowl and make a dressing with the remaining ingredients. Raspberry vinegar will give the salad a sweet taste.

MIXED GRAPEFRUIT SALAD

One grapefruit
Walnut quarters of 8 walnuts
Artichoke hearts (a small jar)
Roasted sweet peppers (½ a small jar)
A bunch of dates
Olive oil and pepper

Peel and cut the grapefruit in sections, remove the pith and mix with all other ingredients. Dress with a little olive oil and pepper.

ORANGE AND GRAPEFRUIT SALAD

One orange
½ grapefruit
½ sweet onion
Olive oil, salt and pepper

Peel and slice the orange and the grapefruit (or cut in wedges). Place in a salad bowl. Prepare the dressing with the thinly sliced onion and pour over the fruit.

DESSERTS

ORANGE CUPS

Four oranges
Two pink grapefruits
Two white grapefruits
60 grams of sugar
Corn starch
Zest of one grated lemon

Scoop the oranges and make cups with handles. Slice two oranges, one pink grapefruit and one white grapefruit and squash with a fork. Squeeze juice of remaining oranges and grapefruits. Mix ¾ of this juice with the sugar and bring to a boil. Add a pinch of corn starch dissolved in hot water and continue boiling until clear; remove from fire and add zest of lemon. Pour over squashed fruit; spoon into orange cups. Refrigerate a few hours and serve with either yogurt or sour cream.

LEMON CUPS

Three eggs
Three tablespoons of sugar
Cornstarch
Juice of one lemon
Grated zest of one lemon

Beat egg yolks until light, add sugar slowly until creamy, then the lemon juice and zest with a pinch of corn starch dissolved in hot water. Beat the egg whites until stiff and fold the mixture into it. Scoop into lemon cups, refrigerate and serve.

LIME MERINGUE PIE

7 tablespoons cornstarch
¾ cup sugar
2 cups boiling water
5 egg yolks
Rind of 2 lemons
¼ cup of limejuice

Sift the cornstarch and sugar in the top of a double boiler. Add the boiling water and stir constantly until thick and creamy.

Stir in five beaten egg yolks, the grated rind and the juice. Cook stirring constantly.

Pour filling into a baked pie shell and cover either with meringue made with the beaten egg whites, bake until browned (15–20 minutes and cool before serving) or decorate with lime slices after baking.

ORANGE CAKE

Three eggs
½ cup sugar
¾ cup flour
Seven spoons of olive oil
Seven oranges
Zest from ½ lemon
Baking soda

Beat the egg yolks until light, add sugar slowly until creamy, add and mix flour and olive oil. Add the juice of the oranges and the lemon zest. Beat the egg white until stiff and fold in the mixture. Pour in a buttered round baking pan and bake in a preheated 350 degree oven for twenty to thirty minutes. When ready decorate with orange slices and serve.

One teaspoon grated lemon rind
¼ cup lemon juice
Five egg yolks
Five egg whites
¾ cup sugar
Powdered sugar
Cream

Sift ¾ cup of sugar and slowly beat in the 5 egg yolks until light colored and creamy. Add one teaspoon grated lemon rind. Add ¼ cup lemon juice. Whisk six egg whites until they form peaks. Fold this in to yolk mixture. Pour the mixture into an oven-proof baking dish, and place this in a larger pan with water. Bake in a 350 degree oven for 35 minutes, or until puffy and golden. Serve with cream.

CRÊPES SUZETTE

The supreme dessert by common consent is crêpes suzette.
    It involves a lot of oranges.
½ cup fresh orange juice
Three tablespoons Grand Marnier ("made with the essence of wild
    tropical oranges")
About three cups orange butter
The outer orange coating only of the skins of 2 navel oranges
½ cup sugar
Two sticks unsalted butter
Eighteen dessert crêpes
One bowl sugar
One bottle Grand Marnier

Purée the orange skins in food processor with ½ cup sugar. Add two sticks unsalted butter; process until creamy. Gradually add ½ cup orange juice. Add three tablespoons Grand Marnier. Pour into bowl and refrigerate.

Dining Room Steps
Light a powerful flame under the chafing dish. Add 3 cups orange butter. Heat for at least five minutes until the mixture bubbles and turns to syrup. Add crêpes individually, immersing both sides. Fold twice into wedges and lay the wedges by edge of chafing dish.

Flambéing
Sprinkle two tablespoons of sugar on crêpes. Pour ½ cup Cognac into ladle and thence on crêpes. Ladle on ⅓ cup Grand Marnier until after a few seconds it bubbles. Ignite by spilling a little of the liquid into the flame. Ladle the flaming liquid profusely onto the crêpes and serve.

Citrus fruits are also used for candied orange peels, chocolate dipped orange peel, and many variations of sweets, sherbets and ice creams.
Marmalade is made commercially. Still, homemade marmalade has a special taste.

You must have very fresh bitter oranges. Cut off the skin, trying to eliminate all the white part, and chop into small pieces. Put aside. Cut the oranges very finely and remove the seeds.

Weigh the oranges, juice and peels.

Weigh the same quantity of sugar. Cook all the ingredients over a medium flame until it thickens, approximately 3 hours, stirring occasionally. Let cool, pack in glass jars, seal and store.

KUMQUAT MARMALADE

2 pounds of kumquats
1 lemon
4 cups sugar
1 ½ quarts of cold water

Slice the fruit and remove the seeds, add water and let stand for 12 hours.

Cook over a low flame until the peel is clear and tender. Add sugar until the marmalade thickens and stir occasionally. Let cool, pack in glass jars, seal and store.

CANDIED GRAPEFRUIT PEEL

2 grapefruits
for each pint of peel (about 2 cups), you will need:
2 cups sugar
1½ cup water
⅛ teaspoon salt
granulated sugar
½ envelope unflavored gelatin (optional)
2 tablespoons cold water

Wash, but do not scrape, peel of grapefruit. (It is the white pith that becomes the good candy.) Cut into strips, cover with water. Bring up to a boil and cook 15–20 minutes, drain and repeat twice more. Bring the sugar, water and salt to a boil, then add peel. Cook slowly, uncovered, until syrup is heavy and almost cooked away, but do not caramelize. When done, remove from heat. At this point unflavored gelatin softened in 2 tablesppons cold water may be stirred in. Remove the peel from the syrup to wax paper. Dry for several hours or overnight. Toss in granulated sugar. Spread on dry wax paper. Dry overnight again. Store in a lightly covered container. Makes about 100 pieces.

Note: Best to prepare on low humidity days. Candy stays good as long as it lasts.

Orange peels drying in the sun for later use in preparing sweets.

ORANGE DRINKS

First you have to make the oranges.
Eat only the orange M&Ms
In each packet. Make friends only
With redheads. Concentrate entirely
On orange juice, which is not the same
  as buying orange juice made from
  concentrate.
Stop looking for the easy way.
Stay focused on your goals.
Visualize all things orange.

Tom C. Hunley

LIMONCELLO

My own favorite pre-dinner drink is that much-loved decoction, limoncello. It delights the Italians, particularly those along the coast south of Naples. You can buy it bottled in America. I recommend getting two or three brands at a time to see which you prefer. Italians who make their own always have their particular secret ingredients, and (particularly in Sorrento) their preferred variety of lemons, but here's an excellent general formulation:

Ingredients
1. A quart of water
2. A quart of alcohol
3. 8 medium-sized entirely organic lemons

Steps
1. Peel the lemons with delicacy and submerge the peels in a jar of alcohol.
2. Close the jar and let stand for four days.
3. Put 2¼ pounds of sugar in a quart of water. Boil until all the sugar is dissolved. Add this syrup to the liquid in the jar and mix.
4. Wait ten minutes, filter and bottle.
5. Serve very cold.

GROG

In any café in France you can get "un grog," which I recommend highly on a bitter day. The usual format is: in a stout glass, place one slice of orange, a clove, sugar, perhaps a bit of cinnamon, and whisky, over which is poured steaming hot water. It raises the outside temperature several degrees and partly brings out the sun.

The name, though, is at least as remarkable as the drink. It is what I call a round-trip word. The French call a particular rough cloth gros grain: "rough surface." This term came into English as grogram. A certain unpopular vice-Admiral Edward Vernon of the Royal Navy usually wore a stout grogram cloak, and was thus called "Old Grog." He fought in the war of Jenkins' Ear and was at the siege of Cartagena, together with George Washington's brother, whence Mount Vernon.

To mitigate their horrible conditions, Royal Navy ships used to dole out a tot of rum to the tars. That resulted in impaired seamanship, including falling off the yards. So Old Grog dictated that the tot be divided between servings and diluted with water, to make it harder to get drunk. The sailors found the resulting insipid beverage disappointing, and called it grog after the unpopular Admiral. Under that name it returned to France, available, as I say, in every café. Try it next time!

hancing chilled plonk than Lafite '45. I say all this as a former Medoc proprietor myself, and thus with a pragmatic approach to the whole subject. ("Rules" about what goes with what, correct glasses and so on, are obsessions of non-professionals.)

VODKA

Some of my White Russian friends put a strip of orange peel in a bottle or carafe of cheap vodka until the contents become faintly straw colored. This provides a charming flavor.

CAMPARI

I am fond of Campari and soda, and kind friends who invite me sometimes keep some around. However, if you look at the label on the back of a Campari bottle you will see recommended two other variations, both of which involve adding a slice of orange. One calls in addition for a generous amount of orange juice. This again amounts to adding fresh orange juice to wine.

BUCK'S FIZZ AND OTHER MATTERS

And consider another such charming mixture, champagne and orange juice: "Buck's fizz" in England or mimosa in the U.S. No one doubts its excellence. As Prince Philip said: "Champagne and orange juice is a great drink. The orange improves the champagne. The champagne definitely improves the orange."

SANGRIA, ETC.

This popular summer drink is made with burgundy, sweetened orange juice, soda, and slices of orange. Then there's the orange blossom: orange juice and vodka. And what about the twist of lemon peel in the dry Martini — a "zeste" as the French call it, from a Greek word for slice. The active ingredient in the peel is called limonine, a different matter from the flavor of the fruit itself. It leaves the pleasant lemony aroma you detect in an empty Coke bottle.

JO FARRAGHER'S INCOMPARABLE ICED TEA

She adds a can of frozen pink (or ordinary) lemonade plus a cup of sugar syrup dissolved in half a cup of hot water.

SHRUB

Patrick O'Brien enthusiasts (of which I am one: I reread the Aubrey-Maturin canon annually) will notice the principals' fondness for shrub, essentially a citrus-based whiskey sour.

ORANGE JUICE WITH WINE

One neglected bit of orange lore may be worth reviving. The ancient Chinese liked orange juice in wine, and the seventeenth century Dutch even more so. At first flush this idea seems rather outré, but in fact the combination is very satisfactory indeed. Everybody I've inflicted it on, including wine fanciers, has loved it.

The Dutch also used to put a peeled orange into a wine glass, like the pear in Poire Williams, but my investigations lead me to prefer just adding the juice.

As usual, fresh juice is preferable to what comes out of a container, and this treatment makes more sense as a way of en-

VARIETIES

ORANGES

This morning I ate an orange.
It is sour and juicy. My mouth
  will tingle all day.
Outside, it is cold. The trees do
  not anticipate their leaves.
When I breathe into my hand I
  smell oranges.

Ronald Wallace

This whole volume would be too small to discuss all the present-day orange varieties, particularly if one included those produced in the commercial farms in America (called "ranches") and elsewhere. There may be almost a thousand. This section describes the most common as well as some unusual varieties.

CITRUS SINENSIS
(Sweet Orange)

CITRUS AURANTIUM
(Bitter Orange)

CITRUS MAXIMA
(Shaddock)

CITRUS LIMON
(Lemon)

CITRUS LIMONIMEDICA
(Ornamental Lemon)

CITRUS MEDICA
(Citron)

CITRUS MEYERI
(Lemon)

CITRUS PARADISI GRANDIS
(Grapefruit)

CITRUS RETICULATA DELICIOSA
(Mandarin and Tangerine)

CITRUS CLEMENTINA
(Clementine)

CITRUS HYSTRIX, CITRUS AURANTIFOLIA
AND MUNMAYA
(Lime)

FORTUNELLA KUMQUAT

CITRUS BERGAMIA
(Bergamot)

CITRUS MYRTIFOLIA
(Chinotto)

One of the four citrus paintings by Bartolomeo Bimbi commissioned by the Medici Family. (See page 24)

Navelina Orchard, Sicily.

ABOVE: *Navel orange.*
BELOW: *Calabrese orange.*

CITRUS SINENSIS ～ SWEET ORANGE

As described in the text, the Portuguese brought this wonderful fruit to Europe from China in the fifteenth century. It is mostly used for table fruit and juice.

Washington Navel orange displays another smaller fruit inside an aperture at its end. (Technically, a second whorl of carpels.) The *Summer navel* is more vigorous. The smaller *Robertson navel* is considered inferior.

Navelina orange and *Wincka* are mostly grown in Sicily.

Valencia, also called *Murcia*, is the most widely disseminated species, primarily used for juice.

Oval or *Calabrese* oranges are mostly used for ornamental purposes.

Jaffa is a large and seedless orange, considered one of the best table fruits.

Cara-Cara was brought to Florida and California from Venezuela.

Foliis Variegatis variegated leaves make this a highly decorative orange.

Mellarosa, a roseapple orange, was found in the Medici gardens in the seventeenth century.

Lumia di Sarzana

Lumia or *Pomum Adami* is a hybrid observed by Marco Polo in Persia .

Other varieties: *Ruby, Honey Bells, Hamlin, Marsh.*

BLOOD ORANGES WITH RED PULP

Moro is a Sicilian medium-sized orange used commercially. *Tarocco* is the largest of the Italian blood oranges. *Sanguinello* is an egg-shaped Spanish orange.

BLOND ORANGE

Portugal is a sweet orange variation.

ABOVE: *Moro oranges.*

RIGHT: *Pomum Adami.*

BELOW: *Lumia di Sarzana.*

Specimens from the Oscar Tintori greenhouse.

Honey bells. (Photo by Camilla McGrath)

ABOVE: *Tarocco.*

BELOW: *Tarocco orange tree. Calabria.*

CITRUS AURANTIUM ∼ BITTER ORANGE

The crusaders are thought to have brought back the bitter orange, used in marmalade, from Palestine. It is very hardy, and can grow entirely outdoors in a mild climate.

Seville, the most common of the bitter oranges.

Bizzaria, the bizarre orange, has green blotches on its skin.

Corniculata, the horned bitter orange, displays odd extrusions on its surface.

Virgatum, called the Swiss orange. This variety is not Swiss at all. Its alternating green and orange stripes suggest the uniform, designed by Michelangelo, of the Papal Swiss guards.

Canaliculata. The fruit of the furrowed bitter orange has vertical folds and somewhat flattened ends.

Crispifolia, the curled leaf orange. Its leaves are oval in shape.

Salicifolia is a willow-leaved Seville orange with long thin leaves.

Turcicum, the Turkish sour orange, seems to be a mutation of the Seville orange, and did indeed come from Turkey. Both its fruit and its long, thin leaf are variegated. Varieties include *Bittersweet, Oklawake, Vek*.

Foliis Variegatis, the Seville orange with variegated leaves, makes an attractive decorative plant.

Foetifera has a disagreeable, lumpy exterior and often reveals a smaller fruit inside the main one.

Seville orange, watercolor by Katherine Manisco.

Seville Caniculata orange, watercolor by Katherine Manisco.

An ornamental orange tree growing by one of the entrances to the Cathedral of Seville.

Seville orange, Casa de Pilatos, Seville.

Seville orange, Generalife castle garden, Granada.

Seville orange, Calabria.

Seville orange tree, Baratti.

ABOVE: *Seville orange grove, Calabria.*

BELOW: *Seville orange. (Photo by Camilla McGrath)*

Virgatum.

Canaliculata.

Crispifolia.

Turcicum.

Salicifolia.

Foliis variegatis.

CITRUS MAXIMA ~ SHADDOCK ORANGE

The shaddock is of South Chinese origin. It is an independent species, like the mandarin and the citron. It is the largest of all oranges and resembles a grapefruit.

Pomelo, also called *Pummelo*.

Melogold and *Oroblanco* are hybrids developed in California.

Chandler is a very large shaddock.

ABOVE: *Pomelo.*

BELOW: *Oroblanco shown with lime for scale. (Photos by Camilla McGrath)*

CITRUS LIMON ~ LEMON

Amalphitanum lemon from Il Pizzo lemon grove, Piana di Sorrento.

CITRUS LIMON ~ LEMON

Originated in southern China and Upper Burma. The Romans brought the fruit to Europe in the first century. It was introduced into Spain by the Arabs. The Crusaders brought the fruit to Europe in 1096. Columbus brought lemon seeds with him on his second voyage to Hispaniola in 1493. The Spaniards brought the lemon to Florida in 1565 and Franciscan fathers to California in 1769.

Florentina lemon flowers and bears fruit year round. Having been cultivated by the Medici from the sixteenth century on, it became favored in Florentine villas generally. It offers abundant, fragrant juice.

Feminello or *Zagara Bianca*. The orange-flower lemon is the one most frequently found in Sicily.

Lunario, or four seasons lemon, flowers and bears fruit year round. Although it only bears fruit when mature, it is then exceptionally productive.

Amalphitanum lemon has an elongated shape and grows on the Amalfi coast.

Canaliculata, a furrowed lemon with quite deep longitudinal exterior striations.

Feminello Carrubaro, found in Sicily, is so named because it looks like the carob, with purple buds and bunched fruits and flowers.

Peretta, a pear-shaped lemon, was cultivated by the Medici in the seventeenth century.

Salicifolia. This willow-leaf lemon has dark, long, narrow leaves, suggestive of a willow's.

Foliis Variegatis, with its yellow and green streaked leaves, is considered exceptionally decorative.

Foliis Variegatis Sanguineum is similar to the above, except that the exterior of the fruit has longitudinal striations.

Eureka is an oval lemon with pronounced stylar and bulge.

Ponderosa or *American Wonder* is an ornamental plant.

Villafranca was imported to Florida by General Stanford.

Bernie lemon grows in Spain.

ABOVE: *Lemon, watercolor by Katherine Manisco.*
BELOW: *Feminello, Calabria.*

ABOVE AND BELOW: *Florentina lemons, Baratti.*

*Terraced lemon
groves, Amalfi.*

Amalphitanum lemon from Il Pizzo lemon grove, Piana di Sorrento.

RIGHT: *Poster for a 19th century citrus vendor.*

FAR RIGHT: *sketch of women in Sorrento.*

DONNE DI SORRENTO

OPPOSITE PAGE: *Lemon Foliis Variegatis Sanguineum.*
Oscar Tintori greenhouse, Pescia.

ABOVE: *Lemon blossom.*

RIGHT: *Eureka lemon, watercolor by Katherine Manisco.*

BELOW: *Ponderosa lemon. (Photo by Camilla McGrath)*

CITRUS LIMONIMEDICA ~ ORNAMENTAL LEMON

Florentine citron was collected for the Medici gardens in the Pietrasanta countryside near Lucca, early in the seventeenth century. Its scent is considered particularly attractive. The fruit has a lengthened tip.

Paradisi is somewhat larger than a lemon, is shaped like an elongated egg, and has thorns.

Maxima, a large-fruited citron, can reach three kilograms, and is a very popular ornamental plant. Its thick skin is good for candying.

Rubra, the red citron, has purple buds and starts out maroon with purple bands, only turning orange as it ripens.

Canarone. This monstrous Florentine citron has a furrow surrounding the protrusion at the bottom.

Rugoso is a wrinkled citron with pale leaves and flowers in spring and autumn.

Perettone. The fruits are pear-shaped with long necks. The leaves shed in winter.

Pigmentata. This red lemon does indeed display a reddish tinge as it ripens. The fruit is excellent.

Bicolore. This Lucca citron has a purply green skin until it ripens completely

Sanctus Dominicus. This small St. Dominic pear-shaped citron may well have been grown by Dominican friars.

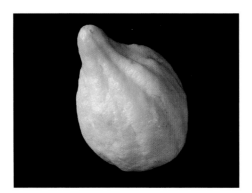

ABOVE: *Limonimedica, Calabria.*

LEFT: *Florentine citron.*
Oscar Tintori greenhouse, Pescia.

Limonimedica, Maxima, Oscar Tintori greenhouse, Pescia.

Limonimedica, Bicolore, Oscar Tintori greenhouse, Pescia.

Limonimedica, Perettone, Oscar Tintori greenhouse, Pescia.

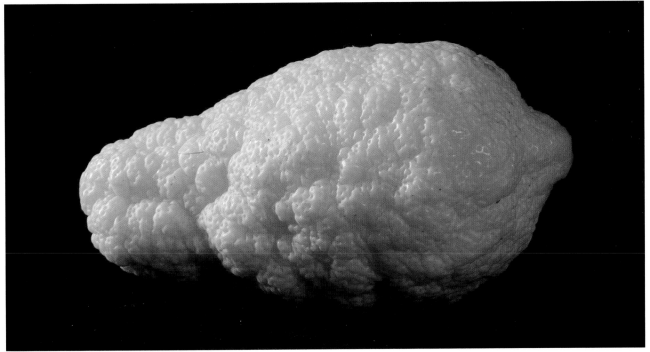

*Limonimedica, Perettone,
Calabria.*

CITRUS MEDICA

Watercolor by Katherine Manisco.

CITRUS MEDICA ~ CITRON

This citron was the first citrus seen in Europe. It apparently reached Italy in the second century BC. Citrons are vulnerable to cold.

Diamante is the most familiar of its species in southern Italy. It is a mutation which arose in Calabria.

Digitata or *The Hand of Buddha* looks like an octopus: a most extraordinary fruit. Each segment is surrounded by its own skin. In the far east it figured in religious ceremonies as a symbol of wealth and happiness. In China and Japan it is used to perfume rooms.

Etrhog or *Israel Citron* originated in Palestine and plays a role in the Hebrew Sukkoth, the Feast of the Tabernacles. It sheds its leaves in winter.

Corsican: of Corsican origin, this fruit is sweet without juice.

Salò. From Lake Garda, this plant eventually spread elsewhere.

Maxima. A highly productive giant citron with a warty exterior. Its fragrant white flowers mostly appear in spring and autumn.

Aurantiata. This Chinese citron is apparently a cross between the citron and the Seville orange. The seedless fruit has a particularly irregular skin.

Crispifolia.

All pictures this and opposite page from the Oscar Tintori greenhouse, Pescia.

ABOVE: *Diamante. Oscar Tintori greenhouse, Pescia.*
OPPOSITE PAGE: *Citrus Medica Maxima.*

BELOW LEFT: *Digitata or The Hand of Buddha on stem.*
BELOW RIGHT: *Digitata, closed fruit, Oscar Tintori greenhouse, Pescia.*

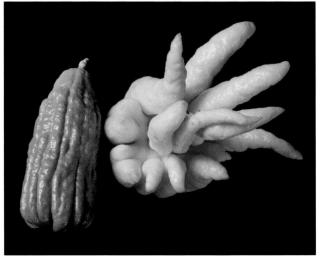

TOP: *Citrus Medica Crispifolia.* ABOVE: *Citrus Medica Etrhog or Israel citron.* RIGHT: *Citrus Medica Aurantiata.*

All specimens are from the Oscar Tintori greenhouse, Pescia.

CITRUS PARADISI GRANDIS
∿ GRAPEFRUIT

Probably a cross between the sweet orange and the pomelo, it was first found in Barbados. The term "grapefruit" may derive from the way the fruits grow in bunches.

Rubra, the star ruby grapefruit, originated in Texas. The essentially seedless fruit has red flesh.

Marsh and *Red Blush* are a medium-sized seedless grapefruit

Duncan is large, very juicy and seedy.

Other varieties are: *Oroblanco, Sweetie, Thompson, Triumph*, etc.

Cross with Mandarin = *Ugli Fruit, Unique* or *Mapo*. Two varieties are *Orlando* and *Minneola*

Cross with tangerine = *Tangelo*

Cross with Clementine = *Mapo*

ABOVE: *Marsh and Red Blush.*

BELOW: *Ugli fruit. (Photos by Camilla McGrath)*

ABOVE RIGHT: *Grapefruit, Sicily.*

BELOW RIGHT: *Grapefruit, Tuscany.*

Citrus Paradisi, watercolor by Katherine Manisco.

CITRUS MEYERI ~ LEMON

The Meyer lemon seems to be an instance of spontaneous cross-breeding between the lemon and the sweet orange. Frank N. Meyer found it in China in 1908 and brought it to America. It stands cold better than the lemon, and flowers and bears fruit year round. Its dark leaves surrounding clusters of flowers give it a handsome appearance.

Volkameriana is perhaps an old hybrid of the lemon and the Seville orange.

Otahite lemon, presumably from Tahiti, is likely to be a cross between a lemon, sweet orange and mandarin. It withstands low temperatures and is very productive.

Citrus paradise or Imperial Lemon is spiny plant and seems to be a handsome cross between a lemon and a grapefruit. Also called *Lipo*.

Cross with sweet orange = *Orange Lemon*
Cross with citron = *Lice*
Cross with Mexican Lime = *Oscar*
Cross with Clementine = *Jambhiri*

(Photo by Camilla McGrath)

CITRUS RETICULATA DELICIOSA ~ MANDARIN AND TANGERINE

The skin of this fruit pulls off readily.

Satsuma. Originated in Japan. It does not hold well on the tree but withstands the cold.

Citrus Reshni, the Cleopatra mandarin, reached America from India toward the end of the nineteenth century. It is highly resistant to cold.

Calamondin or *Chinese Orange,* a decorative plant, which originated in China, can withstand the heat and low humidity of a city residence, and is thus a convenient home decorative element, particularly since it flowers and bears fruit most of the year.

Foliis Variegatis is a particularly decorative version of the foregoing. The skin has green stripes.

Other varities include: *Dancy, King, Honey, Fairchild medium, Cara Cara, Tardivo di Ciaculli, Robinson.*

ABOVE: *Calamondin, watercolor by Katherine Manisco.*
LEFT: *Mandarin, Citrus Reshni. Oscar Tintori greenhouse, Pescia.*
BELOW: *Calamondin. (Photo by Camilla McGrath)*

ABOVE: *Mandarin, Calabria.*

BELOW LEFT: *Foliis Variegatis.* BELOW RIGHT: *Satsuma, Oscar Tintori greenhouse, Pescia.*

Citrus Clementina ~ Clementine

The common Clementine, a hybrid between a mandarin and an orange, may have been named to honor its discoverer, a monk, Clement, who developed it in an orphanage garden on Algeria.

Some varieties are: *Monreal*, *Di Nules* (a new mutation from the Valencia area), *Oroval*, from the same region, and *Tardivo*.

Rubina

Cross with Tangerine and Orange = *Tangor*
Cross with Tangelo, also called Page Orange = *Tangtangello*
Cross with Mapo and Grapefruit = *Carvalhal*
Cross with Sweet Orange = *Mandarancio*

Clementine, Rubina.

Australian Finger Lime, Oscar Tintori greenhouse, Pescia.

CITRUS HYSTRIX, CITRUS AURANTIFOLIA AND MUNMAYA ~ LIME

Native to India, it has a greenish skin which looks as though it was being puffed up into bubbles

CITRUS AURANTIFOLIA ~ SWEET LIME

Messicana, the Mexican or West Indian lime, seems to have been brought to Italy by the Crusaders. It is sensitive to cold. Columbus introduced it to the New World, and Spanish immigrants brought it to Florida, where it got its name "Key Lime."

Neapolitanum, the Neapolitan lime, has juicy seedless flesh.

La Vallette is of Maltese origin.

Limetta is the Mediterranean sweet lime.

Pursha, a Roman lime.

Australian Finger Lime produces both round and cylindrical fruit

Other varieties include: *Rangpur* (an Indian garden plant), *Persian, Bearss Kusay.*

MUNMAYA LIME

Blossoms of Munmaya lime, Oscar Tintori greenhouse, Pescia.

Limetta, Oscar Tintori greenhouse, Pescia.

FORTUNELLA KUMQUAT ~ KUMQUAT

The kumquat or kinkan is of the genus Fortunella, and of the same Rutaceae family as the orange, but is not a true citrus. The plants are particularly hardy. The fruit comes in both oval and round shape.

Margarita or *Nagami*. These kumquats are small and almost spherical; the fruit has a sweet skin and sour flesh.

Hong Kong is tiny and handsome. The fruits remain attached for an unusually long time, which makes the plant attractive for growing in a limited space.

Jiangsu, a sturdier qumkuat with large leaves.

Other varieties: *Kucle* (twice the size of the Margarita) *Meiwa, Golden Bean, Spicy, Japonica*.

Nagami Kumquat. (Photo by Camilla McGrath)

Hong Kong Kumquat. Oscar Tintori greenhouse, Pescia.

CITRUS BERGAMIA ∽ BERGAMOT

The oil in the skin of the bergamot was used by
Giovanni Paolo Feminis to create the original eau
de cologne. Native to Southeast Asia and now
found mainly in Italy, Ivory Coast and Morocco.

Fantastico is a newer, superior, bergamot variation.
The oil from its rind is used in Earl Grey Tea.

Other varieties include *Feminello* and *Castagnaro*.

Oscar Tintori greenhouse, Pescia.

CITRUS MYRTYFOLIA ∽ CHINOTTO

Native to China. The chinotto or myrtle
leaved orange is notable for its small
pointed leaves. It grows very slowly and
makes a good hedge.

Oscar Tintori greenhouse, Pescia.

OTHER VARIETIES

Severinia Buxifolia. The boxthorn's strong leaves resemble the familiar box tree.

Murraya Paniculata or *Jasmine Orange* is a medium-sized ornamental plant. The fruits are tiny and dark orange.

Trifoliate Poncirus orange originated in northern China and withstands cold very well. Alone among all citrus plants it is deciduous; that is, it sheds its leaves annually. Having strong branches armed with powerful thorns, it makes an effective barrier hedge.

Monstruosa or *Flying Dragon* has strange, twisted, horned branches.

Trifoliate Poncirus.

Severinia Buxifolia, Oscar Tintori greenhouse, Pescia.

Alcazares gardens, Seville, Spain.

JOHN TRAIN is author of over twenty books and several hundred columns. Chairman of an investment firm, he has received part-time appointments from three presidents.

MARK E. SMITH is specialized in travel reportage, fine art, nude, archeological and architectural photography.

FOLLOWING PAGE: *A garden in Sorrento. (Photo by Nicholas Sapieha)*